P9-AQE-239

SNOOPY'S

TENNIS BOOK

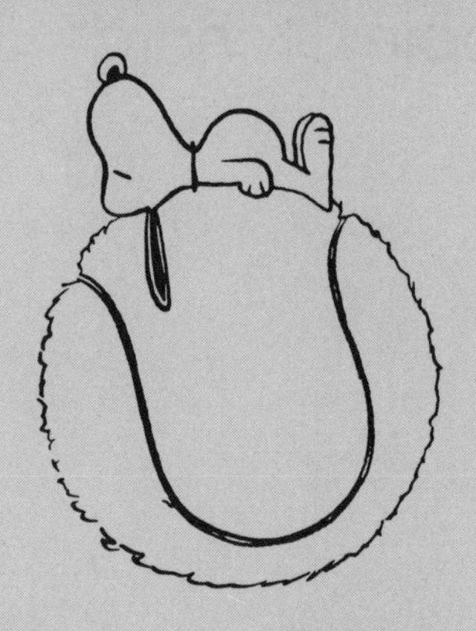

Other Snoopy Books

Snoopy and the Red Baron
Snoopy and His Sopwith Camel
Snoopy and "It Was a Dark and Stormy Night"
Snoopy's Grand Slam
"I Never Promised You an Apple Orchard"

SNOOPY'S
TENNIS BOOK

CHARLES M. SCHULZ

Featuring *Snoopy at Wimbledon* and *Snoopy's Tournament Tips*

INTRODUCTION BY BILLIE JEAN KING

Holt, Rinehart and Winston New York

Copyright © 1979 by United Feature Syndicate, Inc.

All rights reserved, including the right to reproduce
this book or portions thereof in any form.

Published by Holt, Rinehart and Winston,
383 Madison Avenue, New York, New York 10017.

Published simultaneously in Canada by Holt, Rinehart and
Winston of Canada, Limited.

Library of Congress Catalog Card Number: 78-14169
ISBN Hardbound: 0-03-050581-X
ISBN Paperback: 0-03-050585-2

First Edition

Printed in the United States of America
10 9 8 7 6 5 4 3 2 1

Introduction

Like millions of people all over the world, I have followed Snoopy's tennis exploits avidly over the years. I have sympathized with him on those unfortunate but all too frequent occasions when he has been victimized by bad line calls; I have agonized with him when he has been plagued by double-faults or partnered with insensitive, incompetent, or inanimate doubles partners; and I have shared his joy and proud sense of accomplishment when successes, no matter how small, and triumphs, no matter how fleeting, have visited his side of the net.

Perhaps things would be different if he had been born a southpaw, or if he had a second serve that didn't bounce twice before it reached the net, but the fact of the matter is that Snoopy will probably never advance to the top of the rankings. Still, he has served notice that absolutely nothing will prevent him from going out and doing the best he can. Consider his recent trip to Wimbledon.

Though it is the ultimate dream of most tennis players to go to Wimbledon, few ever make it. But despite the overwhelming odds against him, Snoopy finally realized *his* dream when he actually stood on Centre Court's hallowed turf. That historic event is documented here for the first time.

Of course the primary focus of this book

is on his development as a tennis player, but it also includes a particularly illuminating section that offers conclusive proof that Snoopy possesses one of the finest tennis minds the sport has yet produced. If you aren't convinced of this fact now, you surely will be once you have read "Snoopy's Tournament Tips." The advice he offers is insightful, practical, and downright inspired. I only wish that he had shared these bits of wisdom with us years ago.

Anyone who has ever stepped onto a tennis court knows only too well that the game can be as frustrating as it is rewarding, and Snoopy has certainly experienced more than his share of frustrations. But through it all, he has demonstrated a consistently high level of determination, ingenuity, and good humor. His enthusiasm is both contagious and entertaining, which is a winning combination if ever there was one. Perhaps most importantly, this gutsy little athlete has managed to put the game of tennis into proper perspective and to keep it there. He has shown us that the final score really has very little to do with determining who the real winners are.

For these and other reasons too numerous to mention here, Snoopy has rightfully established himself as Everyman's tennis player. He has become an inspiration to all of us, hackers and pros alike.

Hang in there, Snoopy, and don't ever stop swinging away. We need you.

Billie Jean King

GOOD MORNING, PAL!

GOOD MORNING, FUZZY-FACE!

RATS!

NO ONE EVER CALLS ME "PANCHO"!
SCHULZ

ANYONE NEED AN OPPONENT FOR SINGLES?

A FOURTH FOR DOUBLES?

A GUEST FOR LUNCH?
SCHULZ

I HATE IT WHEN THEY RETURN MY SERVE!
SCHULZ

WHAP!

NYAHH! NYAHH! NYAHH!!!

ACTUALLY, AFTER YOU ACE SOMEONE, YOU REALLY SHOULDN'T SAY, "NYAHH, NYAHH, NYAHH!"
SCHULZ

BOUNCE
BOUNCE
BOUNCE

BOUNCE
BOUNCE
BOUNCE BOUNCE
BOUNCE
BOUNCE
BOUNCE
BOUNCE

IT UNNERVES YOUR OPPONENT IF YOU BOUNCE THE BALL A LOT BEFORE YOU SERVE!

HERE'S THE WORLD-FAMOUS TENNIS PLAYER WALKING OUT ONTO THE COURT..

THIS IS THE MOST IMPORTANT MATCH OF THE SEASON...

THIS IS THE BIG ONE! THIS IS IT!!

FIRST SERVE IN?

I APPRECIATE YOUR TAKING ME ALONG TO PLAY TENNIS, LINUS...

THAT'S THE ONLY TROUBLE WITH TENNIS.. YOU CAN'T PLAY IT ALONE

MAYBE WE WON'T GET TO PLAY AT ALL... THE COURTS ARE ALL FULL..

THE COURTS ARE ALWAYS FULL WITH BIG KIDS, AND THEY NEVER LET YOU PLAY... I HATE BIG KIDS! THEY NEVER GIVE YOU A CHANCE!

THEY'LL PLAY ALL DAY....JUST YOU WATCH! THEY'LL HOG THE COURTS ALL DAY! THEY'LL NEVER QUIT...THEY'LL JUST KEEP ON PLAYING AND PLAYING, AND THEY'LL NEVER...

YOU BIG KIDS GET OFF THAT COURT RIGHT NOW, OR MY BOY FRIEND WILL CLOBBER YOU!!

THAT'S THE ONLY TROUBLE WITH TENNIS... YOU CAN'T PLAY IT ALONE
SCHULZ

I'VE BEEN ANXIOUS TO HAVE WOODSTOCK SEE MY NEW RACKET...

HOW DISAPPOINTING...HE HATES MY GUT!
SCHULZ

OVERHEAD SMASH!
SCHULZ

I HOPE HE DOUBLE-FAULTS...

PLEASE DOUBLE-FAULT! DOUBLE-FAULT! DOUBLE-FAULT! DOUBLE-FAULT!

THAT WAS TOO BAD!

RATS!

HE WHO LIVES BY THE LOB DIES BY THE LOB!

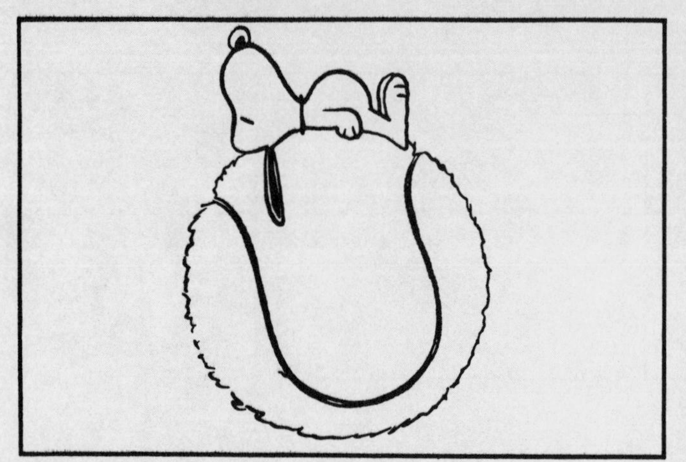

SERVICE!

WHAP!

AAUGHH

BAM!

WANG!

CRUNCH!!

STOMP!
STOMP!
STOMP!
STOMP!

WHAM WAM WHAM
WAM WHAM WAM

AAUGHH!

I HATE IT WHEN I DOUBLE-FAULT!
SCHULZ

OUT ?!!

BAD CALL!

IT HIT THE EXACT MIDDLE OF THE OUTER PART OF THE EDGE OF THE FRONT PART OF THE BACK PART OF THE LINE!
SCHULZ

RATS!

I WOULD HAVE WON, BUT I GOT OFF TO A BAD FINISH!
SCHULZ

PAW FAULT ?!!

WHAM!

RATS!

I SHOULD'VE HAD THAT POINT, AND I SHOULD'VE HAD THAT GAME AND I SHOULD'VE HAD THAT SET...

UNFORTUNATELY, WE'RE NOT PLAYING "SHOULD'VES"!

!

!!

I HAVE A SUGGESTION...LET'S NOT PLAY "FIRST SERVE IN"
SCHULZ

OKAY, HERE COMES THE BIGGIE!

THE BIGGIE WAS A SMALLIE!
SCHULZ

AH!

THIS IS GOING TO BE A GOOD DAY...

I GOT THE NEW CAN OF BALLS OPEN WITHOUT CUTTING MYSELF!
SCHULZ

HA!

I GOT 'IM NOW!

TWO GOOD SERVES AND A COUPLE OF BAD CALLS, AND I'M IN!
SCHULZ

CLANK

THE NEXT TIME YOU SERVE, TAKE THE BALLS OUT OF THE CAN!
SCHULZ

POW!

HE WHO LIVES BY THE POACH DIES BY THE POACH!

RATS!

HOW CAN I SLEEP KNOWING THAT ANY MOMENT A WOLF COULD COME BY, AND BLOW MY HOUSE DOWN?

LIFE HAS TOO MANY WORRIES... TODAY IT'S WOLVES...

YESTERDAY IT WAS MY BACKHAND!
SCHULZ

POW!

QX
!!!!!
SCHULZ

ACED HIM AGAIN!

WHAP!

AAUGH!

I'M SERIOUSLY THINKING OF NOT TAKING MY TENNIS SO SERIOUS...
SCHULZ

I SHOULD HAVE WON TODAY...

I GUESS THE TENNIS GODS WERE AGAINST ME

THAT STUPID WOODSTOCK... HE DOESN'T BELIEVE THERE ARE SUCH THINGS AS TENNIS GODS!
SCHULZ

HE'S BEEN HITTING BALLS AGAINST THAT GARAGE FOR WEEKS...

HE'S PRACTICING FOR A MIXED-DOUBLES TOURNAMENT

OH? WHO'S GOING TO BE HIS PARTNER?
THE GARAGE!
SCHULZ

I HEARD YOU AND THE GARAGE PLAYED IN A MIXED-DOUBLES TOURNAMENT

HOW DID YOU COME OUT? DID YOU PLAY WELL?

I PLAYED GREAT...

BUT THE GARAGE CHOKED!
SCHULZ

HITTING BALLS AGAINST THE GARAGE AGAIN, I SEE...

I FIND IT INTERESTING THAT YOU SHOULD HAVE THE GARAGE FOR A PARTNER WHEN YOU PLAY MIXED-DOUBLES

I WAS ALSO WONDERING WHAT THE BEST PART OF HIS GAME IS...

HE NEVER FOOT-FAULTS!

REALLY? HOW DISAPPOINTING

NO GAME TODAY...

WOODSTOCK HAS "TENNIS WING"!

HERE'S SOMETHING YOU SHOULD THINK ABOUT WHEN YOU'RE PLAYING TENNIS

KNOW WHAT KIND OF BALL YOU'RE PLAYING AND WHAT NUMBER IS ON IT SO YOU WON'T GET MIXED UP WITH THE PLAYERS NEXT TO YOU

MINE HAS A LITTLE SNOWMAN ON IT...
THAT'S A NUMBER EIGHT

ANYONE FINDS A BALL WITH A SNOWMAN ON IT, IT'S MINE!!!
SCHULZ

HERE'S A TENNIS TOURNAMENT YOU SHOULD ENTER...

AFTER THE TOURNAMENT IS OVER, THEY'RE HAVING A BIG BANQUET

I NEVER ATTEND TENNIS BANQUETS
SCHULZ

IF I LOSE, I'M ALWAYS TOO MAD TO EAT!

OUT!!

OUT!

OUT!

OUT?!

HE WHO LIVES BY THE BAD CALL, DIES BY THE BAD CALL!
SCHULZ

STILL HITTING BALLS WITH THE GARAGE, I SEE...

IT'S GOOD PRACTICE..HE GETS EVERYTHING BACK

I WAS SURPRISED YOU DIDN'T PLAY DOUBLES AT WIMBLEDON THIS YEAR..

THE GARAGE HATES TO FLY
SCHULZ

BANG
BANG
BANG

ALL RIGHT, WHO'S OUT THERE MAKING ALL THAT NOISE?

IT'S THE GARAGE
BANG
BANG
BANG
BANG

HE KEEPS HITTING 'EM BACK!
SCHULZ

HITTING BALLS AGAINST THE GARAGE MUST BE GOOD PRACTICE...

IT'S PROBABLY ALSO FUN, ISN'T IT?

UNTIL SOMEONE PARKS THE CAR!

A TENNIS PRO ONCE SAID THAT YOU COULDN'T BE A CHAMPION UNTIL YOU HAD HIT TEN THOUSAND BALLS AGAINST THE GARAGE

THAT WASN'T A TENNIS PRO...

THAT WAS A GARAGE SALESMAN!
SCHULZ

WHAT'S THE SCORE?

WE'RE BEHIND, FIVE-THREE?

NOT TO WORRY, PARTNER... NOT TO WORRY!

WE'LL BREAK THIS GUY'S SERVE, THEN WE'LL WIN YOUR SERVE, THEN WE'LL BREAK THE OTHER GUY'S SERVE, THEN I'LL GIVE 'EM FOUR BIGGIES AND WE'LL BE IN!

OKAY, PARTNER?

HE AGREES WITH EVERYTHING EXCEPT THE FOUR "BIGGIES"!
SCHULZ

PRACTICING FOR THE DOUBLES TOURNAMENT I SEE...

I SUPPOSE YOU AND THE GARAGE WILL BE PARTNERS AGAIN...

I DON'T THINK SO

HE DOESN'T MOVE AS WELL AS HE USED TO!
SCHULZ

GUESS WHAT..

THEY'VE POSTED THE TEAMS FOR THE MIXED DOUBLES TOURNAMENT

YOU KNOW WHO YOUR PARTNER IS? MOLLY VOLLEY!

MOLLY VOLLEY?
SCHULZ

SEE?

YOU DREW MOLLY VOLLEY FOR A PARTNER IN THE MIXED DOUBLES...

IN THE LAST TOURNAMENT SHE BEAT UP HER PARTNER, TWO LINESMEN AND A BALL BOY!

HERE SHE COMES NOW..
ALL RIGHT, WHERE'S MY PARTNER?
SCHULZ

HI, I'M MOLLY VOLLEY!

HI, MY NAME IS CHARLIE BROWN

THIS IS SNOOPY...HE'S GOING TO BE YOUR PARTNER IN THE TOURNAMENT

I'VE HEARD OF MIXED DOUBLES, BUT THIS IS RIDICULOUS!
SCHULZ

OKAY, "PARTNER"..

LET'S GET A FEW THINGS STRAIGHT... I HATE TO LOSE!

I'LL MAKE ALL THE LINE CALLS AND TAKE ALL THE OVERHEADS! ALL YOU HAVE TO DO IS GUARD YOUR ALLEY!

AND JUST ONE SMART REMARK ABOUT MY FAT LEGS GETS YOU A KNOCK ON THE NOGGIN!!
SCHULZ

HERE'S SOMETHING TO THINK ABOUT, PARTNER..

THE FIRST TIME YOU DOUBLE FAULT, I'M GONNA HIT YOU RIGHT OVER THE HEAD WITH MY RACKET!

OKAY, GO AHEAD AND SERVE! AND DON'T BE NERVOUS...

SCHULZ

OUT!

YOU HEARD ME!! I SAID IT WAS OUT!! YOU WANT ME TO SPELL IT FOR YA?!

EVERY BALL YOU GUYS HAVE HIT HAS BEEN OUT! EVERY BALL **WE'VE** HIT HAS BEEN **IN**!!!

HANG IN THERE, PARTNER, WE'RE GONNA **WIN**!!
SCHULZ

MINE!!

WHAP!

GOOD TEAMWORK, PARTNER! WE'RE GONNA **WIN**!
SCHULZ

OUT!

WADDYA MEAN, ARE WE SURE? WE CALLED IT OUT, DIDN'T WE?

YOU CALL YOUR SIDE, AND WE'LL CALL OURS! OUT IS OUT! QUIT STALLING! HIT THE BALL!

THAT'S TELLING 'EM, PARTNER!! WE'RE GONNA WIN!!
SCHULZ

HOW'S THE MATCH GOING?

I THINK SNOOPY AND MOLLY VOLLEY JUST WON THAT GAME...

IT WAS OUT! IT WAS OUT BY FORTY FEET! WHAT IS IT WITH YOU? CAN'T Y'SEE?!
SCHULZ

AT LEAST THEY'VE WON ALL THE ARGUMENTS...

PUT IT AWAY, PARTNER! PUT IT AWAY!

BLAP!
AAUGH

WHEN YOU HIT A VOLLEY, IT'S SUPPOSED TO GO "THONG!" NOT "BLAP!"

BLAP! GOOD GRIEF!
SIGH
SCHULZ

WELL, THAT'S THE FIRST SET, PARTNER...

YOU'RE PLAYING VERY WELL, MOLLY...
I'M IN THE ZONE, KID!

IF MY PARTNER, HERE, DOESN'T BLAP ANY MORE PUT-AWAYS, WE'LL WIN!

YOU'RE NOT GONNA BLAP ANY MORE PUT-AWAYS, ARE YOU, PARTNER?
I WOULDN'T THINK OF IT!
SCHULZ

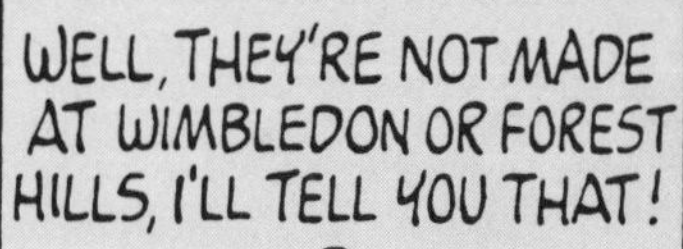

THEY'RE MADE RIGHT HERE ON THESE DIRTY, BUMPY, MISERABLE COURTS WHERE YOU CALL YOUR OWN LINES AND KEEP YOUR OWN SCORE!

SEE THAT FAT LADY OVER THERE?

SHE'S THE MOTHER OF ONE OF THE KIDS WE'RE PLAYING...

SHE COMES TO SEE THAT HER LITTLE DARLING GETS GOOD CALLS! SHE HATES ME

SHE KNOWS THAT WHEN I'M PLAYING, ALL THE CALLS ARE GOING TO BE IN CENTIMETERS!
SCHULZ

HOW'S THE MATCH GOING NOW?

THEY JUST TIED THE THIRD SET...THEY'RE GOING TO PLAY A TIE-BREAKER...
WOW!

OKAY, PARTNER...IT'S TIME FOR A WORD OF ENCOURAGEMENT...

DON'T DO ANYTHING STUPID!!!
SCHULZ

IT'S THREE TO FOUR IN THE TIE-BREAKER..

MINE!

WAP!

FOUR-ALL IN THE TIE-BREAKER!
SCHULZ

WHERE'S THE BALL?

I LOST IT IN THE SUN! WHERE DID IT GO? DID YOU SEE IT?

DID IT GO OUT?! WAS IT IN, OR WAS IT OUT? DID WE WIN, OR DID WE LOSE?

DON'T JUST STAND THERE! CALL IT IN, OR CALL IT OUT!!
SCHULZ

YOU CALL IT, PARTNER!
WAS IT IN OR OUT? DO WE WIN OR LOSE?

IN!

SORRY, PARTNER!
SMAK!

AAUGH!!
SCHULZ

I'M PROUD OF YOU, SNOOPY..

THAT WAS A GOOD CALL YOU MADE EVEN THOUGH IT COST YOU THE MATCH...

THAT'S THE ONLY WAY TO PLAY THE GAME

BESIDES, I KNEW IT WAS GETTING NEAR SUPPERTIME
SCHULZ

WHAP!

WHAP!

I DIDN'T INVENT THE DOUBLE FAULT... I MERELY PERFECTED IT!
SCHULZ

DOUBLE FAULT!

JOE CHOKE
SCHULZ

I HEAR YOU'RE THINKING OF PLAYING AT WIMBLEDON THIS MONTH

I MIGHT...

I HAVE TO FIND OUT MORE DETAILS

I WONDER IF YOU HAVE TO BRING ALONG A CAN OF BALLS...
SCHULZ

HEY, STUPID CAT! I'M THINKING OF GOING TO WIMBLEDON..

WHY DON'T YOU COME ALONG? IF I BREAK A STRING, I MAY NEED SOME EXTRA CAT GUT!!

SLASH!

HOW ABOUT MOUSE GUT?
SCHULZ

IF I'M GOING TO WIMBLEDON, I SHOULD FIND OUT WHERE IT IS...

I'VE ALWAYS HAD AN IDEA IT WAS NEAR KANSAS CITY...

IF YOU'RE LOOKING FOR WIMBLEDON, IT'S IN ENGLAND
REALLY?

I WAS SORT OF COUNTING ON A LAYOVER IN KANSAS CITY...
SCHULZ

ARE YOU SURE YOU WANT TO PLAY AT WIMBLEDON?

YOU'D PROBABLY COME UP AGAINST PLAYERS LIKE ASHE, OR CONNORS, OR OKKER OR BORG...

THAT'S TRUE... I HATE PLAYING GUYS LIKE THAT

THEY KEEP HITTING THE BALL BACK!
SCHULZ

WHERE WILL YOU STAY IF YOU GO TO ENGLAND?

YOU DON'T KNOW ANYONE THERE

WHY CAN'T I STAY DOWNSTAIRS WITH MR. HUDSON AND MRS. BRIDGES?

BETTER YET, I'LL STAY UPSTAIRS WITH MISS GEORGINA!
SCHULZ

I ENVY YOU GOING TO ENGLAND

YOU'RE GOING TO HAVE A GREAT TIME... YOU'LL LIKE THE FOOD, TOO...

YOU CAN HAVE KIDNEY PIE EVERY NIGHT FOR DINNER!

MAYBE I'LL STAY HOME
SCHULZ

?

YOU'RE LEAVING FOR WIMBLEDON NOW?

BUT IT'S THE MIDDLE OF THE NIGHT!!

YOU ALWAYS LEAVE FOR WIMBLEDON AT NIGHT... IF YOU LOSE IN THE FIRST ROUND, NO ONE WILL EVER KNOW
SCHULZ

WHERE'S YOUR DOG GOING IN THE MIDDLE OF THE NIGHT?

HE'S GOING TO WIMBLEDON
TO PLAY TENNIS?

GOOD LUCK, SNOOPY!!

CALL LOTS OF FOOT FAULTS!
SCHULZ

THAT DOG OF MINE CAUSES ME MORE WORRY!

NOW, HE'S OFF TO WIMBLEDON...AT LEAST HE THINKS HE'S OFF TO WIMBLEDON...HE DOESN'T EVEN KNOW WHERE IT IS!

HOW IN THE WORLD DOES HE THINK HE'S GOING TO GET THERE?

♪ I BEEN WORKIN ON THE RAILROAD... ♪
SCHULZ

SNOOPY AT WIMBLEDON

Know your way around London
WIMBLEDON?

WIMBLEDON? ANYONE GOING TO WIMBLEDON?

Southfields
I WAS LUCKY... I GOT KICKED OFF THE TRAIN AT THE RIGHT PLACE!

IT'S HARD TO SERVE WHEN THE GRASS TICKLES YOUR FEET...

I BEAT EVERT IN PRACTICE TODAY...NOT CHRIS...HER MOTHER!

FREW AND I HAD THIS DISCUSSION, SEE, SO I SAID TO HIM, "OKAY, I'LL PLAY YOU FOR YOUR CAP!"

I WAS AFRAID THIS WOULD HAPPEN..I CAN'T PLAY ON CENTER COURT BECAUSE I DIDN'T BRING A CAN OF BALLS!

I'VE HAD A GOOD DAY.. I ATE TWELVE BOWLS OF STRAWBERRIES AND CREAM, AND I FELL IN LOVE WITH LINKY BOSHOFF!

HEY, STUPID CAT... PUTTING ON A LITTLE WEIGHT, AREN'T YOU?

YOU SHOULD TAKE UP TENNIS... YOU ALREADY HAVE THE GUT!

SLASH!

AND A WICKED FOREHAND!
SCHULZ

A PRESENT? FOR ME?

I LOVE GETTING PRESENTS

WOW! JUST WHAT I NEED...

A DOZEN FOREHAND VOLLEYS!
SCHULZ

SNOOPY

OUT!!

SMASH!

KILL!!

DRIVE!

SLAM!
SMACK!

OUT!!

SMASH!

KILL! KILL! KILL!!

SMASH!

NICE GAME!
SCHULZ

THIS ACTUALLY HAPPENED

OR AT LEAST IT COULD HAVE

THERE WAS THIS GIRL NAMED POOCHIE, SEE...

WELL, POOCHIE WAS A REAL GOOD TENNIS PLAYER...

SHE PLAYED DOUBLES A LOT, AND YOU KNOW WHAT EVERYONE USED TO SAY ?

"LET'S GO OVER, AND WATCH POOCHIE POACH!"

HEE HEE
HEE HEE
HEE HEE

KLUNK!
KLUNK!

LAUGHING IS GOOD FOR YOU IF YOU DON'T KILL YOURSELF
HEE HEE HEE HEE
SCHULZ

ARE YOU READY TO PLAY?

OKAY...SPIN FOR SERVE!

THAT ISN'T EXACTLY WHAT I MEANT..
SCHULZ

HOLD IT! THERE'S A BUG CROSSING THE COURT!

C'MON, BUG, HURRY UP BEFORE YOU GET STOMPED ON...

WHAT'S THAT? OH.... ALL RIGHT, THANK YOU...

HE SAID I SHOULD BEND MY KNEES MORE
SCHULZ

HE HAS TENNIS ELBOW?

I HAVE A STRAP THAT MIGHT HELP

TELL HIM TO WEAR IT THE NEXT TIME HE PLAYS...

I HAVE MY DOUBTS, BUT I'LL TRY ANYTHING
SCHULZ

I'M SURE THIS LETTER IS FROM MY BROTHER SPIKE IN NEEDLES...

IT MUST BE IMPORTANT... IT HAS A THIRTEEN CENT STAMP ON IT!

THE NAME ON THE STAMP SAYS CARL SANDBURG...

THAT'S GOTTA BE PANCHO GONZALES!
SCHULZ

TOP
SEEDED

OKAY, PARTNER.. THE SECRET TO BEING A GOOD DOUBLES TEAM IS COOPERATION!

IF I SAY, "CROSS OVER!" YOU RUN TO THE OTHER SIDE IMMEDIATELY!

IF I SAY, "YOURS!" YOU TAKE IT... IF I SAY, "MINE!" THEN I'LL TAKE IT...

OKAY? LET'S SHOW 'EM HOW!

POW!
YOURS!
SCHULZ

IF YOU'RE GONNA FOOL ME WITH A DROP SHOT, YOU'LL HAVE TO DISGUISE IT BETTER THAN THAT!

SCHULZ

I HATE PLAYING ON A WINDY DAY!!
SCHULZ

HOLD IT! THERE'S A BUG CROSSING THE COURT!

HURRY UP, YOU STUPID BUG! DO YOU WANNA GET STEPPED ON? C'MON, YOU'RE HOLDING UP THE GAME!

WHAT?

LOVE-THIRTY... WE'RE FOUR-ALL IN THE FIRST SET!
SCHULZ

HOLD IT! HERE COMES THAT BUG ACROSS THE COURT AGAIN..

WHAT? NO, THIS ISN'T HIGHWAY TWELVE...THIS IS A TENNIS COURT...

HIGHWAYS ARE BLACK... TENNIS COURTS ARE GREEN..

IT WAS THE STRIPE DOWN THE MIDDLE THAT CONFUSED HIM.......SERVICE!!
SCHULZ

OH, GOOD GRIEF... A LOB!

I HOPE IT GOES OUT!
I HOPE IT GOES OUT!

I HOPED IT OUT!
SCHULZ

AAUGH!! THIS GAME DRIVES ME CRAZY!

HAVE YOU EVER CONSIDERED SWITCHING TO A METAL RACKET?

NEVER!

A METAL RACKET HURTS WHEN YOU BITE IT!
SCHULZ

Please proceed to your next lesson.

We are very pleased with your progress.
?

A CORRESPONDENCE COURSE?! IN TENNIS?!?

HOW IN THE WORLD CAN YOU STUDY TENNIS BY MAIL?
LESSON III

SIMPLE! WE READ THE TEXTBOOKS CAREFULLY...
LESSON IV

WE STUDY PHOTOS...
WE TAKE QUIZZES..

AND EVERY AFTERNOON WE GO DOWN TO THE CORNER...

SCHULZ
..AND HIT BALLS AGAINST THE MAILBOX!
US MAIL

DEUCE?! WHAT DO YOU MEAN, DEUCE?
MOLLY VOLLEY

YOU'RE SERVING TO ME!

YOU'RE WRONG! THE SCORE IS THIRTY-FORTY! IT WAS LOVE-FIFTEEN AFTER I HIT THAT BEAUTIFUL CROSSCOURT VOLLEY...

THEN, WHEN MY PARTNER HIT THAT MISERABLE BACKHAND INTO THE NET, IT WAS FIFTEEN-ALL!

THEN I HIT THAT PERFECT LOB RIGHT ON THE BASELINE TO MAKE IT FIFTEEN-THIRTY...

THEN MY PARTNER MISSED THAT COLD PUT-AWAY AT THE NET WHICH MADE IT THIRTY-ALL!

THEN I HIT A TOPSPIN BACKHAND JUST LIKE A BULLET RIGHT DOWN THE LINE! THE SCORE IS THIRTY-FORTY!

WE KNOW THE SCORE, DON'T WE PARTNER?
SIGH
SCHULZ

I WOULD LIKE TO THANK EVERYONE FOR THIS FINE TOURNAMENT WE HAD HERE TODAY..THE FANS.. THE LINE JUDGES...

AND, OF COURSE, THE BALL BIRDS!
SCHULZ

MOLLY VOLLEY'S ON THE PHONE
NOW WHAT?

SHE WANTS TO KNOW IF YOU'D BE INTERESTED IN ANOTHER MIXED-DOUBLES TOURNAMENT ON SUNDAY...

I DOUBT IT...

I'VE HAD DISTEMPER, AND I'VE PLAYED MIXED-DOUBLES... I'D RATHER HAVE DISTEMPER
SCHULZ

MOLLY VOLLEY JUST CALLED

SHE SAID THE MIXED DOUBLES TOURNAMENT STARTS TOMORROW

YOU GUYS PLAY "CRYBABY" BOOBIE IN THE FIRST ROUND

"CRYBABY" BOOBIE ?!
SCHULZ

I'VE PLAYED AGAINST "CRYBABY" BOOBIE BEFORE! IT'S AN EXPERIENCE!

HER BROTHER, BOBBY BOOBIE, DOESN'T SAY MUCH, BUT SHE COMPLAINS ABOUT EVERYTHING

JUST DON'T LET HER GET TO YOU...JUST LET IT ALL GO IN ONE EAR AND OUT THE OTHER...

THAT'S THE SPIRIT, PARTNER!
SCHULZ

OKAY, WE'LL RECEIVE ON THIS SIDE
THAT'S NOT FAIR!

THAT MEANS WE HAVE THE SUN IN OUR EYES! WHY DO WE ALWAYS SERVE WITH THE SUN IN OUR EYES?!

SEE? DIDN'T I TELL YOU? "CRYBABY" BOOBIE COMPLAINS ABOUT EVERYTHING!
SCHULZ

I THINK THE NET IS TOO HIGH! THESE BALLS FEEL DEAD! I CAN'T PLAY ON A SLOW COURT! THESE BALLS ARE TOO LIVELY! I THINK THE NET IS TOO LOW!

HEY, "CRYBABY," WHY DON'T YOU SHUT UP AND SERVE?

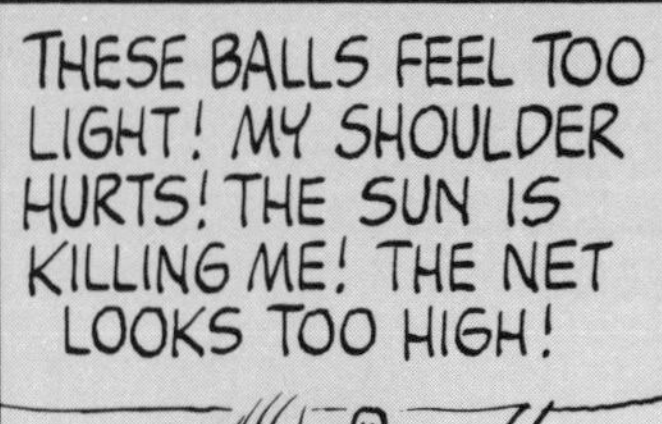
THESE BALLS FEEL TOO LIGHT! MY SHOULDER HURTS! THE SUN IS KILLING ME! THE NET LOOKS TOO HIGH!

I SAID, "SHUT UP AND SERVE!"

NOW YOU'RE TRYING TO PSYCHE ME OUT!!
SCHULZ

FAULT!

FAULT?! THAT WAS A BAD CALL! THAT BALL WAS IN! HOW COULD YOU CALL IT OUT? YOU'RE CHEATING ME!

SHUT UP, "CRYBABY" BOOBIE, AND SERVE!

THIS IS GOING TO BE A LONG DAY!
SCHULZ

HONK!
ALL RIGHT, "CRYBABY," TELL YOUR MOTHER TO CUT IT OUT!

SHE SITS THERE IN HER CAR, AND EVERY TIME YOU MAKE A GOOD SHOT, SHE HONKS THE HORN!

THE NEXT TIME SHE DOES THAT I'M GONNA TEAR OFF A WHEEL!

I COULD HAVE STAYED HOME AND GOTTEN INTO A NICE GENTLE DOGFIGHT
SCHULZ

HOW'S THE TENNIS MATCH GOING?
"CRYBABY" BOOBIE AND HER BROTHER ARE LEADING

WHO'S HONKING THAT CAR HORN?
THAT'S "CRYBABY'S" MOTHER

EVERY TIME HER DAUGHTER HITS A GOOD SHOT, SHE HONKS THE HORN

WILL YOU CUT THAT OUT?!
YOU DON'T LIKE MY MOTHER!
SCHULZ

ALL RIGHT, PARTNER, IT'S MATCH POINT...

WE HAVE TO CONCENTRATE! THAT'S THE SECRET, PARTNER! CONCENTRATE!

I GOT A LETTER FROM MY BROTHER, SPIKE, TODAY...

HAS ANYONE EVER NOTICED THAT THE PORTRAIT OF CARL SANDBURG ON A THIRTEEN-CENT STAMP LOOKS LIKE PANCHO GONZALES?
SCHULZ

"ACE!"

AAUGH!

WE WON!!!

HONK! HONK! HONK! HONK! HONK! HONK!
I'M GONNA KILL SOMEBODY!
SCHULZ

IT'S MATCH POINT, AND YOU STAND THERE LOOKING AT A LETTER FROM YOUR STUPID BROTHER!

NO WONDER YOU GOT ACED!

NOW WE HAVE TO GO AND CONGRATULATE "CRYBABY" BOOBIE! THIS IS GONNA KILL ME!

NICE MATCH, GUYS! LA DE DA DE DA DE DA
SCHULZ

BEATEN BY "CRYBABY" BOOBIE! WHAT A BLOW!

NOW I HAVE TO CONGRATULATE HER..

I DON'T KNOW WHY I PLAY THIS GAME..

CONGRATULATIONS, BOOBIE!
!
SCHULZ

DOWN THE CENTER STRIPE..

SERVICE!

ACE!

WHAT DO YOU MEAN, IT WASN'T AN ACE?

IF IT WASN'T AN ACE, WHAT WAS IT?

2 ♣

HEE HEE HEE HEE HEE
SCHULZ

blap!

DOUBLE FAULT?!

AAUGHH!

SMASH!

WANG

BOOT!

STOMP STOMP
STOMP STOMP

WHAP!

CRASH!

Gentlemen,
Under seperate cover I am returning a defective tennis racket.
SCHULZ

Snoopy's Tournament Tip #1

When filling out the entry blank, make certain you place yourself in the proper category.

Snoopy's Tournament Tip #2

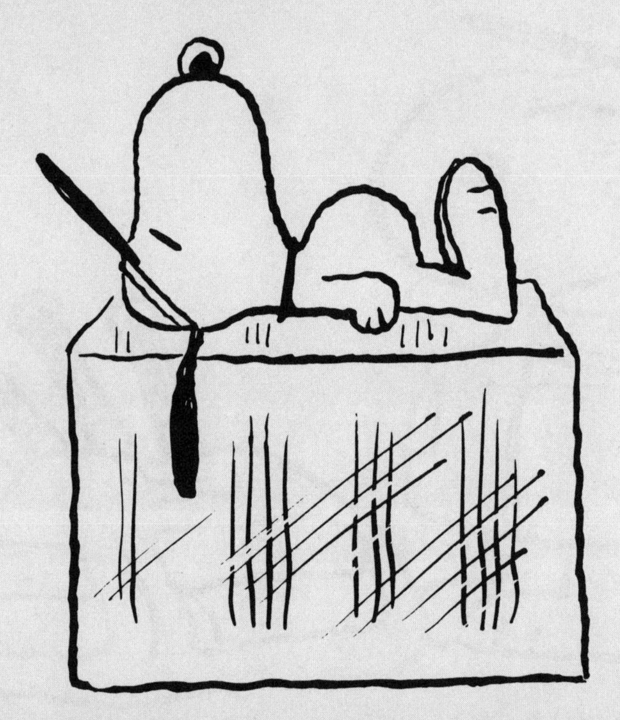

After a strenuous practice session you may want to pack your arm in ice . . . (or, preferably, your whole body).

Snoopy's Tournament Tip #3

Some people are easily impressed by clothing and equipment . . .
therefore, a flashy warm-up jacket and several extra rackets can be important.

Snoopy's Tournament Tip #4

Always offer to open a new can of tennis balls, but do it as slowly as reaching for a dinner check. If care is taken, one unopened can should last the entire season.

Snoopy's Tournament Tip #5

During the warm-up, ask your opponent if you may hit a few overheads, but do so knowing that he'll find out you don't really have an overhead.

Snoopy's Tournament Tip #6

It is considered improper to
bounce the ball excessively so as to annoy the receiver,
but go ahead and try it anyway.

Snoopy's Tournament Tip #7

It is not necessary to argue about
a suspected bad call . . .
sometimes a slight look of dismay
will do the trick.

Snoopy's Tournament Tip #8

If your opponent has a hard first serve, don't let it bother you . . .
if he or she has a hard second serve, you can let *that* bother you.

Snoopy's Tournament Tip #9

It is always wise to bring along something to drink between sets.

Snoopy's Tournament Tip #10

If your opponent runs you from side to side,
avoid obvious signs that you are tiring.

Snoopy's Tournament Tip #11

It is admirable to try to run down every shot, but also unwise to attempt grandstand plays that could cause foolish injury.

Snoopy's Tournament Tip #12

Remember, in playing singles, you actually have no one to blame your losses on but yourself . . . therefore, you may want to take up doubles.

Snoopy's Tournament Tip #13

When playing doubles, refrain from saying anything if your partner hits a cold put-away into the net.

Snoopy's Tournament Tip #14

If your partner double faults four times in a row,
you may want to suggest that he or she throw the ball higher . . .
or take up bowling!

Snoopy's Tournament Tip #15

If you have won, always approach the net graciously
to congratulate your opponent on a match well played.

Snoopy's Tournament Tip #16

If you have lost, always approach the net graciously
to congratulate your opponent on a match well played.

Snoopy's Tournament Tip #17

And remember, once a match is over and you have returned home, it is probably too late to call a serve "out."